OUR HOLY FAITH

OUR HOLY FAITH

BOOK TWO

LAMB OF GOD

TAN Books
Gastonia, North Carolina

Originally published in 1960 as Our Holy Faith Book II: Jesus Comes by Bruce Publishing Company and reprinted in 1998 by The Neumann Press.

Nihil Obstat:

John F. Murphy, S.T.D.

Censor Librorum

Imprimatur:

William E. Cousins

Archbishop of Milwaukee

November 13, 1959

This TAN Books edition has been re-typeset and enhanced with additional content and revisions, including modernized language and updates to the practices of the Catholic Church. Catechism questions and answers have been replaced with the TAN edition of The Third Council of Baltimore: Baltimore Catechism 1–4.

Scripture quotes are adapted from the Douay-Rheims 1899 American Edition.

Content revisions and updates by Elisa Torres
Interior design by Caroline Green
Interior illustrations by Jordan Avery
Cover design by www.davidferrisdesign.com

Cover image: The Ghent Altarpiece, detail of Adoration of the Lamb by Jan van Eyck. Public domain via Wikimedia Commons

ISBN: 978-1-5051-1921-3

Published in the United States by
TAN Books
PO Box 269
Gastonia, NC 28053
www.TANBooks.com

Printed in the United States of America

Contents

Publisher's Note

The original editions of the *Our Holy Faith* series textbooks were published between 1959 and 1964. They were compiled by many different authors over the course of several years. Consequently, the texts varied in their organization from year to year, with similar sections appearing with different names throughout the series and often in varying sequences.

For greater ease of use and consistency, we have reorganized each book so that the Catechism lessons, tests, and other exercises are placed at the end of each relevant chapter or lesson. We have also included answer keys for your convenience in the back of each book.

While the teachings in the original editions remain relevant due to the enduring truths of our Faith, it was necessary to update other aspects in order to more accurately reflect the Church today. These new editions have been revised to incorporate some of the changes to the practices of the Catholic Church.

To the extent possible, we have adapted the text to reflect both the ordinary and extraordinary forms of the Mass and liturgical calendars. In addition to these updates, we have inserted, where relevant to the text, traditional prayers and quotes from the Bible, the Catechism, and the saints.

This new Our Holy Faith series is faithful to the work of the original authors. It honors the fundamental and unchanging truths of the Catholic Church and is heavily influenced by tradition. We believe it is the catechesis you can trust with your children's faith.

UNIT

1 Our Heavenly Father Takes Care of Us

CHAPTER 1
God

God is my heavenly Father.
God made me to show His goodness and to make me happy with Him in heaven.
He gave me my body, my soul, my life.
All that I am or do is God's gift.
I belong to God.

God gave me my father and my mother.
God gave me my brothers and sisters.
He gives me everything I need.
God takes care of me all the time.
I love God because He is so good to me.

I will thank Him for all His goodness to me.
I want to know more about God.
I want to love Him more.
I will give myself and my work to Him each day.

One day, with God's help, I will go to my true home in heaven.
In the meantime, I will live heaven on earth by doing the will of God.
As we pray in the Our Father, "Thy will be done on earth as it is in heaven."

Catechism Lesson

1. Who is God?
God is the Creator of heaven and earth and of all things.

2. Who made you?
God made me.

3. Why did God make you?
God made me to show His goodness and to make me happy with Him in heaven.

4. What must you do to be happy with God in heaven?
To be happy with God in heaven I must know Him, love Him, and serve Him in this world.

5. Who will help me get to heaven?
God will give me all the help I need to get to heaven.

CHAPTER 2
God's Creations

God is everywhere.
God knows all things.
God can do all things.
No one is greater than God.
There is no one like God.
God always was and God always will be.

There is only one God.
In God there are three Divine Persons:
God the Father, God the Son, and God the Holy Spirit.
We call these three Persons in one God the Blessed Trinity.
I believe that there are three Persons in one God because God has told us so.
I think of the three Divine Persons each time I make the Sign of the Cross.

When I make the Sign of the Cross carefully, I praise God.
I will bless myself and say slowly: "In the name of the Father, and of the Son, and of the Holy Spirit. Amen."

Catechism Lesson

6. Where is God?
God is everywhere.

7. Does God know all things?
Yes, God knows all things.

8. Can God do all things?
Yes, God can do all things.

9. Did God have a beginning?
No, God had no beginning; He always was.

10. Will God always be?
Yes, God will always be.

11. Is there only one God?
Yes, there is only one God.

12. How many Persons are there in God?
In God there are three Persons—the Father, the Son, and the Holy Spirit.

13. What do we call the three Persons in one God?
We call the three Persons in one God the Blessed Trinity.

14. How do we know that there are three Persons in one God?
We know that there are three Persons in one God because we have God's word for it.

CHAPTER 3

Angels

God made the angels.

We do not see angels because they are spirits.

Spirits do not have bodies as we do.

Angels are powerful and have great knowledge.

Good angels are in heaven with God.

Good angels sometimes come to earth with messages from God.

Good angels praise God in heaven and on earth.

The angels who did not obey God are called bad angels or devils.

These bad angels chose hell.

These bad angels suffer very much.

They do not like us because we are God's children.

Bad angels try to make us disobey God.

Good angels help us to love and obey Him.

Good angels who watch over us are called guardian angels.

Our guardian angels help us to love and obey God.

Catechism Lesson

15. Who made the angels?

God made the angels.

16. What are angels?

Angels are spirits created by God.

17. Why did God make the angels?

God made the angels to love and adore Him.

18. Did all the angels stay good?

No, some of them disobeyed God and were sent to hell.

19. Where did the good angels go?

The good angels went to heaven with God.

20. What do the angels do in heaven?

The angels love and praise God in heaven.

21. What do the bad angels do in hell?

The bad angels suffer and hate God.

22. What do the good angels do on earth?

The good angels watch over us, pray for us, and sometimes bring messages from God.

23. What do the bad angels do on earth?

The bad angels try to harm us by tempting us to do wrong.

CHAPTER 4

God Our Creator and Saviour

A long, long time ago there was no one but God.
There were no angels.
There was no world.
There were no animals.
There were no plants or trees.
There were no men.
There was only God.
But God was not lonely.
He was very happy.
God does not need anything to make Him happy. He is happiness.
God is good; because He is good He wants to share His happiness with us.

To show His goodness and to share it with us God made:
- the day and night
- the sky
- the water and land
- the sun, moon, and stars
- the plants and the trees
- the fishes and birds
- the animals and man.

God made these things by His almighty power.
All things belong to God.

God watches over all things.
All people belong to God.
I belong to God.
God watches over me.
God watches over all people in the world.
Adam and Eve were our first parents.
When God made them He gave them many gifts.

Adam and Eve lost these gifts when they disobeyed God.
Their sin was the first sin on earth.
God punished Adam and Eve for their sin.
Adam and Eve were no longer God's adopted children, and they lost many gifts God had given them.
But God promised to send them a Saviour.

I came into this world without sanctifying grace. This kind of grace is a sharing in God's life.
I was born with sin on my soul.
This sin is called original sin.
Everyone, except Jesus and His Mother, comes into this world with this sin.

God sent His only Son, Jesus Christ, to be the Saviour.

That is, He sent Him to free us from sin and give us grace.

God the Son became man to save us from hell and win for us His Father's pardon.

He became man to help everybody to gain heaven.

Jesus offered His sufferings and death to God in satisfaction for the sins of men.

The Saviour, Jesus Christ, brought back to men the great gifts God had once given them.

Jesus founded the Catholic Church to help all men gain heaven.

Catechism Lesson

24. Did God make all things?

Yes, God made all things.

25. Who were the first man and woman?

The first man and woman were Adam and Eve.

26. Where did God place Adam and Eve?

God placed Adam and Eve in the Garden of Paradise.

27. What did God do for Adam and Eve?

God gave Adam and Eve many gifts to make them very happy.

28. What did God tell Adam and Eve not to do?

God told Adam and Eve not to eat of the fruit of a certain tree that grew in the Garden of Paradise.

29. Who committed the first sin on earth?

Our first parents, Adam and Eve, committed the first sin on earth.

30. What happened to Adam and Eve when they disobeyed God?

When Adam and Eve disobeyed God they sinned and lost many of their gifts.

31. Is this sin passed on to us from Adam?

Yes, this sin is passed on to us from Adam.

32. What is this sin in us called?

This sin in us is called original sin.

33. Is Jesus Christ both God and man?

Yes, Jesus Christ is both God and man.

34. Why did God the Son become man?

God the Son became man to satisfy for the sins of all men and to help everybody to gain heaven.

35. How did Jesus satisfy for the sins of all men?
Jesus satisfied for the sins of all men by His sufferings and death on the cross.

36. How does Jesus help all men to gain heaven?
Jesus helps all men to gain heaven through the Catholic Church.

37. Was anyone ever free from original sin?
The Blessed Virgin Mary was free from original sin.

UNIT

2 How Some People Obeyed God

CHAPTER 5
The Obedience of Noah

Some of the children of Adam and Eve obeyed God.
Others forgot God and disobeyed Him.
They were sinful.
These bad people made God very angry.
He punished them by sending a great flood.

One man obeyed and pleased God.
This man's name was Noah.
God wanted to save Noah.
God told Noah how to build a great boat or ark.
Noah did what God told him.
When the ark was made God told Noah to go into it.
He told Noah to take his family and every kind of animal into the ark.
Noah obeyed God.
Then God sent the great flood.
The people outside the ark drowned.
The animals outside the ark drowned.
Those in the ark were saved.
Noah offered a sacrifice (a gift) to God to thank Him for saving him and his family.

God was pleased.

God promised Noah that He would never again destroy people by the waters of a flood.

He put the rainbow into the sky to show that He would be true to this promise.

Catechism Lesson

38. Who was Noah?

Noah was a holy man who lived before Jesus Christ came to earth.

39. Why was God pleased with Noah?

God was pleased with Noah because Noah obeyed God.

40. What did God tell Noah to do?

God told Noah to build an ark.

41. Why did God tell Noah to build an ark?

God told Noah to build an ark to save himself and his family from the flood.

42. Why did God send the flood?

God sent the flood to punish the bad people.

43. How did Noah thank God for saving him and his family?

Noah built an altar and offered sacrifices to God.

44. What did God promise Noah?

God promised Noah that He would never again destroy man by a flood.

CHAPTER 6
The Obedience of Abraham

Abraham was a holy man who lived many years before Jesus Christ came on earth.

Abraham believed everything God told him.

Abraham loved and obeyed God.

God was very pleased with Abraham.

He told Abraham to leave his home and go into the land which He would show him.

Abraham obeyed God and always trusted Him.

One day God asked Abraham to do something very hard. He wanted to test him.

God wanted to see whether Abraham loved Him above all things, even more than his only son, Isaac.

He asked Abraham to offer his only son, Isaac, as a sacrifice.

Abraham made everything ready to offer his son.

But God saved Isaac.

He gave Abraham an animal to sacrifice in place of Isaac.

Abraham proved that he did indeed love God above everything.

God blessed Abraham.

God promised Abraham that he would be the father of the Chosen People.

The Chosen People were the Hebrews.

God promised Abraham that the Saviour of the world would come from them.

Catechism Lesson

45. Who was Abraham?

Abraham was the father of God's Chosen People.

46. Why did God choose Abraham to be the father of his People?

God chose Abraham because he was obedient and holy.

47. What did God tell Abraham to do?

God told Abraham to leave his home and to go to the land which God would show him.

48. How did God test Abraham's obedience?

God told him to sacrifice his son, Isaac.

49. How did God show that He was pleased with Abraham?

God saved Isaac and promised Abraham that he would be the father of the Chosen People.

CHAPTER 7
The Obedience of Moses

Moses was a holy man chosen by God to work for Him.
God called Moses in a special way.
Moses heard the voice of God in a burning bush.
God told Moses who He was.
Then God gave Moses work to do for Him.
God told Moses to lead the Chosen People out of Egypt to the Promised Land.
Moses said that he was afraid.
God promised to give Moses all the help that he would need.
Moses did everything God told him to do.

Catechism Lesson

50. Who was Moses?

Moses was a holy man chosen to do great work for God.

51. What work did God give Moses to do?

God told Moses to lead the Chosen People out of Egypt to the Promised Land.

52. How did God give this command to Moses?

God appeared to Moses in a burning bush.

CHAPTER 8
The Obedience of Samuel

Samuel was a holy child.
God gave him to his mother because she prayed so hard for a son.
His mother, Hannah, gave Samuel to God.
Hannah sent him to live in the tent where the Chosen People kept the Ark of the Covenant.
This was a box which contained the stone tablets on which God wrote the Ten Commandments.
Samuel worked for God there.
God was very pleased with Samuel.
One night God awakened Samuel and talked to him.
He asked Samuel to do something hard for Him.
God told Samuel to tell Eli, the high priest, about his sinful sons.
Samuel did what God told him to do.
God rewarded Samuel for his obedience.
He made Samuel a great teacher and ruler of the Chosen People.

Catechism Lesson

53. Who was Samuel?

Samuel was a holy child who loved God and worked for Him in the tent where the Ark of the Covenant was kept.

54. Who spoke to Samuel in the tent?

The Lord God spoke to Samuel in the tent.

55. What did God tell Samuel to do?

God told Samuel to warn the priest Eli that his sons were committing great sins.

56. Did Samuel answer God's voice?

Yes, Samuel obeyed God even though it was hard for him to do so.

57. Why was it hard for Samuel to obey?

It was hard for Samuel to obey because Samuel was afraid to tell Eli about his sinful sons.

58. Did God reward Samuel for his obedience?

Yes, when Samuel was older, God made him a great teacher and the ruler of the Chosen People.

CHAPTER 9

The Obedience of the Holy Family

One day God kept His great promise to send His Son.

A wonderful thing happened to the Blessed Virgin Mary.

God sent His angel to visit her in Nazareth. The angel's name was Gabriel.

The angel told Mary that God wanted her to be the Mother of His Son.

Mary believed the angel.

Mary said she was willing to carry out God's plan and become the Mother of Jesus.

We call Mary's Son Jesus Christ.
Jesus is God.
Jesus is a man, too.
Jesus is both God and man.
Jesus is the second Person of the Blessed Trinity.
Jesus was born in a stable in Bethlehem on the first Christmas Day.
Each Christmas, we celebrate the birthday of Jesus.
Jesus is God.

Mary is the Mother of Jesus.
Mary is the Mother of God.
Saint Joseph is the foster father of Jesus. Saint Joseph is the true husband of Mary.
We call Jesus, Mary, and Joseph the Holy Family.

Jesus loved His Father in heaven.
He always obeyed His Father and loved His Mother Mary.
He loved Saint Joseph, His foster father.
Jesus always obeyed Mary and Joseph.
Mary and Joseph, too, did everything to please God.
Our family also pleases God when we obey Him as the Holy Family did.
The Holy Family lived in Nazareth.
Jesus stayed at His home in Nazareth until He was about thirty years old.

Then Jesus began to do the work which His Father had given Him to do.

His work was to teach. He was to save all people. He was to lead them to heaven.

Day after day Jesus went around doing good.

Jesus healed sick people.

He brought some dead people back to life again.

Most of all, He saved men from sin and made them children of God.

Some people disobeyed Jesus.

Some people did not like Jesus.

They laughed at Jesus.

They wanted to kill Jesus.

Jesus loved all people.

Jesus suffered for all people.

Jesus died for all people.

He died for our sins on a cross.

Jesus died on Good Friday.

Jesus died so that all people could live with him forever in heaven.

Since Jesus died on the cross, many holy people have loved and served him.

Many of these good people are now in heaven with God.

These holy people are called saints.

Some of these saints were little boys and girls.

We can learn from these little saints how to love and obey God.

Catechism Lesson

59. Who is the Mother of Jesus?
The Mother of Jesus is the Blessed Virgin Mary.

60. Who told the Blessed Virgin Mary that she was to be the Mother of Jesus Christ?
The Angel Gabriel came from heaven with this message to the Blessed Virgin Mary.

61. What did the angel tell the Blessed Virgin Mary?
The angel told the Blessed Virgin Mary that she was to have a Son who would be the Son of God.

62. Was the Blessed Virgin Mary willing to be the Mother of God the Son?
Yes, the Blessed Virgin Mary was willing to carry out God's plan and become the Mother of Jesus.

63. Did one of the Persons of the Blessed Trinity become man?
Yes, the second Person, the Son of God, became man.

64. What is the name of the Son of God made man?
The name of the Son of God made man is Jesus Christ.

65. When was Jesus born?
Jesus was born on the first Christmas Day, more than two thousand years ago.

66. Is Jesus Christ really God?
Yes, Jesus Christ is really God.

67. Is Jesus Christ really man?
Yes, Jesus Christ is really man.

68. Is Jesus Christ both God and man?
Yes, Jesus Christ is both God and man.

UNIT

3 How We Should Obey God

CHAPTER 10
The First Commandment

God gave the Ten Commandments to us through Moses.
He gave them to Moses on Mt. Sinai.
They were written on tablets of stone.

The Ten Commandments are:

1. I am the Lord thy God; thou shalt not have strange gods before me.
2. Thou shalt not take the name of the Lord thy God in vain.
3. Remember thou keep holy the Lord's Day.
4. Honor thy father and thy mother.
5. Thou shalt not kill.
6. Thou shalt not commit adultery.
7. Thou shalt not steal.
8. Thou shalt not bear false witness against thy neighbor.
9. Thou shalt not covet thy neighbor's wife.
10. Thou shalt not covet thy neighbor's goods.

We must all obey these ten laws of God.
When I obey these laws I show God that I love Him.
God made me to be happy with him in this life and in heaven.
I want to be close to God now and with Him in heaven forever.
These ten laws of God will help me get to heaven.
They show me the way.

The first law of God tells me that I must love God above all things.

I love God:

when I say my morning and night prayers every day.
when I go to Mass.
when I think of Him during the day.
when I tell Him how sorry I am that I disobeyed Him.
when I ask God to forgive my sins,
when I ask God for His help.
when I thank God for everything that He has given me.
when I love my brothers and sisters.
when I obey my parents.
I break God's first law:
if I miss my morning or night prayers for a long time.
if I purposely think of other things while praying.
if I love myself more than God.

Catechism Lesson

69. Besides believing in God what else must I do to get to heaven?

Besides believing in God, I must keep His commandments.

70. To whom did God give the commandments?

God gave the Ten Commandments to us through Moses.

71. What is the first commandment of God?

The first commandment of God is: I am the Lord thy God; thou shalt not have strange gods before me.

72. What does the first commandment tell me to do?

The first commandment tells me to adore God and to pray to Him.

73. What does the first commandment forbid me to do?

The first commandment forbids me:

1. to miss my morning or night prayers for a long time through laziness or shame.
2. purposely to think of other things while praying.

CHAPTER 11

The Second Commandment

God's name is holy.

It is holier than all other names.

I honor God's name when I use it with faith and love.

I should bow my head when I speak or hear the name of Jesus.

God wants me to use His name in the right way.

I use God's name in the right way when I pray to Him.

I also use God's name right when I tell others about Him.

I must try never to use God's name in the wrong way.

I offend God when I do this.

I honor God's name when I say the Divine Praises.

Catechism Lesson

74. What is the second commandment of God?

The second commandment of God is: Thou shalt not take the name of the Lord thy God in vain.

75. What does the second commandment tell me to do?

The second commandment tells me:

1. to honor the name of God.
2. to respect holy persons, holy places, and holy things.

76. What does the second commandment forbid me to do?

The second commandment forbids me:

1. to use the holy name of God carelessly or in anger.
2. to dishonor holy persons, holy places, and holy things.

CHAPTER 12
The Third Commandment

Sunday is the Lord's Day.

I must keep this day holy because God told me to.

The Lord's Day is a very holy day because Christ rose from the dead on a Sunday.

The Catholic Church teaches me how to keep this day holy.

I keep God's day holy when I attend Holy Mass.

The Holy Sacrifice of the Mass pleases God more than anything else.

I can please God in these ways too:

1. By praying to God using my own words.
2. By reading an uplifting story.
3. By taking a nature walk so as to enjoy the beauty of creation.
4. By doing good works such as:
   Helping mother at home.
   Being kind to others.
   Visiting my sick friends.

I will go to Mass every Sunday and holy day.

I will never miss Holy Mass on Sundays or holy days unless I have a very good reason.

On Sunday I will come to Holy Mass on time.

I will not talk or look around in God's house.

I will stay for the whole Mass.
God is kind to me.
He does not want me to work all the time.
God wants Sunday to be a day of rest.
God forbids me to do all unnecessary work on that day.
How kind God is to give me a day for prayer, rest, and play.

Catechism Lesson

77. What is the third commandment of God?

The third commandment of God is: Remember thou keep holy the Lord's Day.

78. What does the third commandment tell me to do?

The third commandment tells me to assist at Holy Mass on Sundays and holy days.

79. What else should I do to keep Sunday holy?

I should say extra prayers, read something holy, and do good works.

80. What does the third commandment forbid me to do?

The third commandment forbids me:

1. to miss Holy Mass on Sundays and holy days through my own fault.
2. to come late to Holy Mass on these days through my own fault.
3. to misbehave in Church.
4. to do work that is not necessary on Sundays.

CHAPTER 13
The Fourth Commandment

God in His goodness gave me my parents.
My parents love and care for me.
They teach me to love and serve God.
God wants me to love and obey my parents.
God wants me to love and obey priests and my teachers.
God wants me to love my parents even when they are old or sick.
Jesus taught me how to love and obey my parents.
He wants me to be as good to them as He was to Mary and Joseph.
I will try to do as Jesus did.

Catechism Lesson

81. What is the fourth commandment?

The fourth commandment of God is: Honor thy father and thy mother.

82. What does the fourth commandment tell me to do?

The fourth commandment tells me to love, honor, and obey my parents and all those who take their place.

83. What does the fourth commandment forbid me to do?

The fourth commandment forbids me:

1. to disobey my parents and all those who take their place.
2. to talk back to my parents.
3. to be mean and to make fun of my parents or my elders.

CHAPTER 14

The Fifth Commandment

God is my Father.

I am God's child.

God wants me to love everyone and to be kind to everyone.

When I love others, and am kind to them, I show God that I love Him.

God told me that I must not hurt anyone.

I should be like Jesus, meek and patient.

I must not fight or quarrel.

I must not keep mean thoughts about others in my mind.

I should try to do good for others by words and by actions.

I must not lead others to do anything wrong.

If I keep this commandment of God, I will make myself and others happy.

Catechism Lesson

84. What is the fifth commandment of God?

The fifth commandment of God is: Thou shalt not kill.

85. What does the fifth commandment tell me to do?

The fifth commandment tells me:

1. to be kind to everyone.
2. to help others do what is right.
3. to take proper care of my health.

86. What does the fifth commandment forbid me to do?

The fifth commandment forbids me:

1. to be angry or stubborn.
2. to fight or quarrel.
3. to keep mean thoughts about others in my mind.
4. to lead others to do wrong.

CHAPTER 15

The Sixth and Ninth Commandments

God has put many wonderful things in this world for me.

God gave me a mind to know Him.

God gave me a heart to love Him.

God gave me a body to serve Him.

Therefore, I must keep my mind, heart, and body pure and clean.

God wants me to be pure in all I think, do, or say.
God hates bad thoughts.
God hates bad words.
God hates bad pictures, bad shows in the movies or on the TV or internet.
God hates bad actions.
God loves pure little boys and girls.
They are God's dearest children.

Catechism Lesson

87. What is the sixth commandment?

The sixth commandment is: Thou shalt not commit adultery.

88. What is the ninth commandment?

The ninth commandment of God is: Thou shalt not covet thy neighbor's wife.

89. What do these commandments tell me to do?

These two commandments tell me to be pure and modest in all I think, do, or say.

90. What do these two commandments forbid me to do?

These two commandments forbid me:

1. to think purposely of impure things.
2. to look purposely at impure pictures.
3. to speak purposely impure words.
4. to do purposely impure things alone or with others.

CHAPTER 16
The Seventh and Tenth Commandements

God wants me to enjoy the things He created.

He forbids others to take what belongs to me, and He forbids me to take what belongs to them.

Taking anything that belongs to someone else is stealing.

I must try to return things that I find, and always return things that I borrow.

I must have respect for other people's belongings.

I offend God when I steal.

If I help others to steal, I also offend God.

I break God's seventh commandment when I steal.

I must give back whatever I take.

God forgives me when I give back what I took.
When I copy other children's work, I steal.
This is called cheating.
Cheating is a sin.
I offend God when I cheat.
Even when I simply "wish" to steal or cheat, I commit a sin.
I should be satisfied with the things that I have.
God gave me all the things I have.
God gave me my parents.
I please God when I am happy with the things that He has given me.
I will thank God every day for all His wonderful gifts to me.

Catechism Lesson

91. What is the seventh commandment of God?

The seventh commandment is: Thou shalt not steal.

92. What is the tenth commandment of God?

The tenth commandment of God is: Thou shalt not covet thy neighbor's goods.

93. What do these two commandments tell me to do?

These two commandments tell me:

1. to respect the property of others.
2. to be content with what is our own.

94. What do these two commandments forbid me to do?

These two commandments forbid me:

1. to steal and cheat.
2. to keep anything that is not mine.
3. to break other people's things on purpose.
4. to keep things that were borrowed or found.

CHAPTER 17

The Eighth Commandment

God wants me to tell the truth at all times.
I must tell the truth when I talk about myself.
I must tell the truth when I talk about others.
I must not tell the faults of others.
God is not pleased when I say things that are mean or are wrong about others.
I must never tell a lie.
God hates a lie.
God Himself is Truth.
We become more like God when we speak the truth.

Catechism Lesson

95. What is the eighth commandment of God?

The eighth commandment of God is: Thou shalt not bear false witness against thy neighbor.

96. What does the eighth commandment tell me to do?

The eighth commandment tells me:

1. to tell the truth at all times.
2. to think and speak kindly of others.

97. What does the eighth commandment forbid me to do?

The eighth commandment forbids me:

1. to tell lies.
2. to think and say mean things about others.
3. to tell lies about others.
4. to keep unkind thoughts about others in my mind.

CHAPTER 18

The Laws of the Church

The Catholic Church is the true Church of Jesus Christ.
He is its Head.
Christ gave us His Church so that by it He might give divine life to all men.
I belong to the Catholic Church.
If I remain faithful to the Church, I will be close to Christ.
I am a member of His Body.
The Catholic Church shows me the way to heaven.
The Catholic Church tells me what I must know and do to please God.
Jesus speaks to me through the Church.
Because He does, I must believe all the things that the Catholic Church teaches me.
I must do all things that the Catholic Church teaches me to do.
I must obey the five precepts of the Church.
I please God when I keep the precepts of His Church.
The five precepts of the Catholic Church are these:
You shall attend Mass on Sundays and holy days of obligation.
You shall confess your sins at least once a year.
You shall receive the sacrament of the Eucharist at least during the Easter season.
You shall observe the days of fasting and abstinence established by the Church.

You shall help to provide for the needs of the Church.

We will learn these precepts of the Church by heart when we are older.

Catechism Lesson

98. What laws of the Church must I keep?

1. I must attend Mass on Sundays and holy days of obligation.
2. I must not eat meat on the days appointed by the Church.
3. I must give generously of what I have, whether money or service time.

UNIT

4 How God Pardons Sin

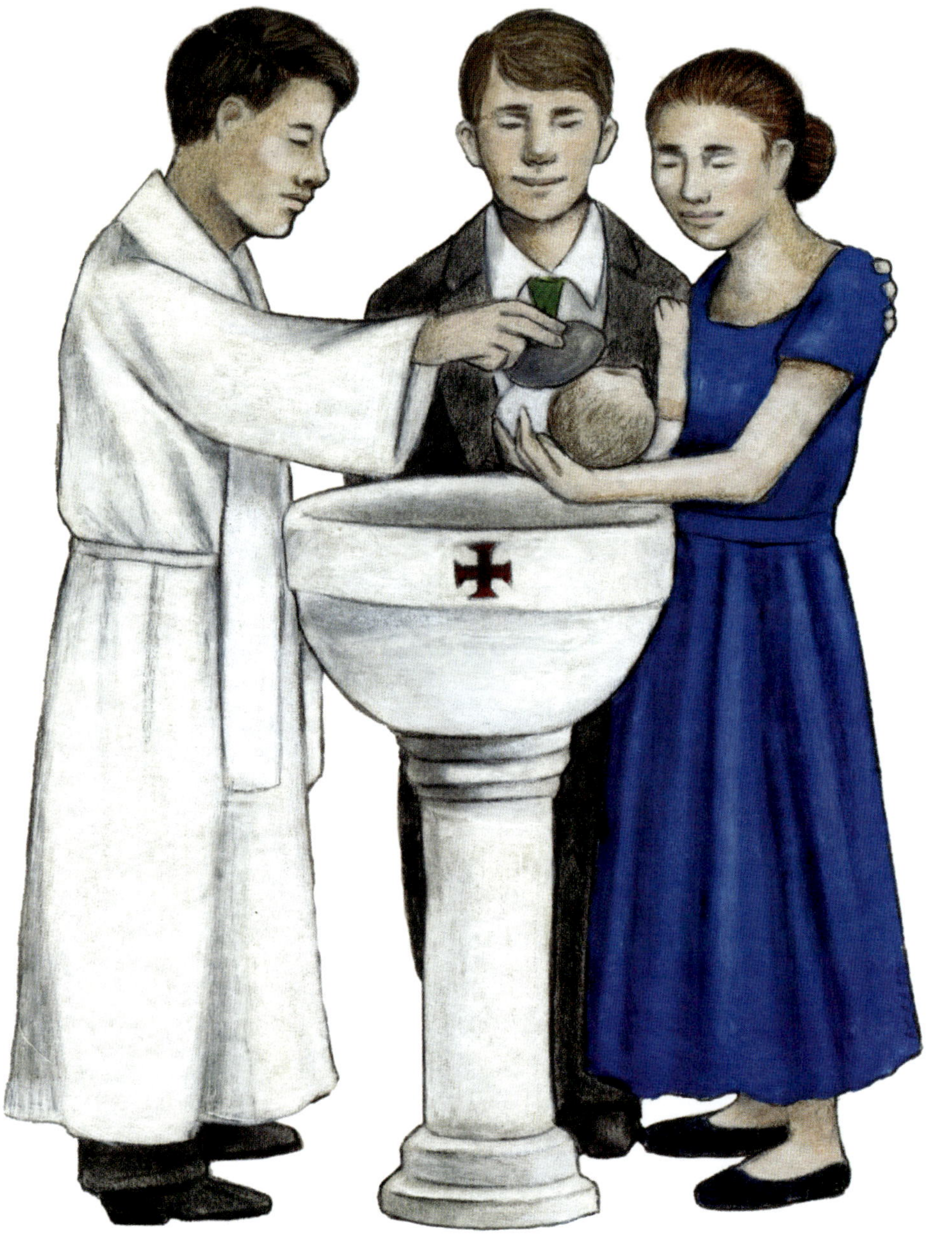

CHAPTER 19
The Sacrament of Baptism

Christ gave the Church seven signs to help her members receive grace. These seven signs are called the seven sacraments.

Baptism is the first of these sacraments.

It takes away original sin and makes me a child of God and a member of His Church.

Penance and Reconciliation takes away my sins and gives me grace to do good.

Holy Eucharist gives me Jesus as the Food of my soul.

Confirmation brings the Holy Spirit to me and makes me a soldier of Jesus Christ.

Holy Orders makes a man a priest of God.

Matrimony makes a man and woman husband and wife and brings them closer to Christ.

Anointing of the Sick gives me God's grace when I am in danger of death.

I came into this world with the sin of Adam.

This sin in me is called original sin.

When I was baptized original sin was taken away.

I became a child of God.

God came to live in me, giving me a share in His life.

This life of God in me is called grace.

Catechism Lesson

99. How does the Catholic Church help us to gain heaven?

The Catholic Church helps us to gain heaven especially through the sacraments.

100. What is a sacrament?

A sacrament is an outward sign, instituted by Christ to give grace.

101. Which sacrament do I receive first?

I receive the sacrament of Baptism first.

102. What is Baptism?

Baptism is a sacrament that gives our souls the new life of grace by which we become children of God.

103. Why do I receive the sacrament of Baptism first?

I receive the sacrament of Baptism first because Baptism takes away original sin and makes me a child of God.

104. Who baptizes us?

The priest baptizes us.

105. Can anyone else baptize?

Yes, if you cannot get a priest, any Christian may baptize.

106. How would you baptize?

I would baptize by pouring ordinary water on the forehead of the person to be baptized, saying while I was pouring it: "I baptize you in the name of the Father, and of the Son, and of the Holy Spirit."

Prayer for the Renewal of Baptismal Vows

Let us renew the promises made for us at our Baptism:

Priest:	Do you renounce Satan?
CHILDREN:	I do renounce him.
Priest:	And all his works?
CHILDREN:	I do renounce them.
Priest:	And all his empty promises?
CHILDREN:	I do renounce them.
Priest:	Do you believe in God, the Father Almighty, Creator of heaven and earth?
CHILDREN:	I do believe.
Priest:	Do you believe in Jesus Christ, His only Son, our Lord, who was born, and who suffered for us?
CHILDREN:	I do believe.
Priest:	Do you also believe in the Holy Spirit, the Holy Catholic Church, the communion of saints, the forgiveness of sins, the resurrection of the body, and life everlasting?
CHILDREN:	I do believe.
Priest:	Now stand and say the Apostles' Creed.
Priest:	Kneel and say the Our Father.

CHAPTER 20
Sin

When I break God's law I commit a sin.

Any sin that I commit is called an actual sin. There are two kinds of actual sin:

1. Mortal sin, a great offense against God.
2. Venial sin, a lesser evil.

When I commit a mortal sin I choose to become an enemy of God; I cut myself off from God's divine life within me. If I die in a state of mortal sin I will have chosen to go to hell forever.

Missing Holy Mass through my own fault on Sunday is a grave sin.

If I know what I am doing is a grave sin and I continue to commit the sin freely, I commit a mortal sin.

Venial sin is not a full rejection of God.
But venial sin offends God too.
Venial sin weakens God's life in me.
Stealing a dime, or telling a little lie, or disobeying my teachers would be a venial sin.
God hates all sin.
I must hate all sin.
Sin makes me sad.
God wants me to be happy in this life.
I must be sorry for my sin if I hope to be happy now and in heaven.
I will ask God to help me keep away from all sin.
God will help me do this.

Catechism Lesson

107. What is sin?

Sin is disobedience to God's laws.

108. What is actual sin?

Actual sin is any sin we ourselves commit.

109. How many kinds of actual sin are there?

There are two kinds of actual sin: mortal sin and venial sin.

110. What is mortal sin?

Mortal sin is a grave sin that we commit knowingly and freely.

111. What does mortal sin do to us?

Mortal sin makes us enemies of God and robs our souls of His grace.

112. What happens to those who die in mortal sin?

Those who die in mortal sin have chosen to be punished forever in hell.

113. When is a sin mortal?

A sin cannot be a mortal sin unless:

1. The sin is *grave*.
2. I *know* that it is grave before I do it.
3. I *want* to do it.

114. What is venial sin?

Venial sin is a lesser sin.

115. Does venial sin displease God?

Yes, venial sin does displease God.

116. When is a sin venial?

A sin is venial when:

1. The sin is *not grave*.
2. When the sin is grave but you think it is *not grave*.
3. When the sin is grave but you do not really *want* to do it.

CHAPTER 21
The Sacrament of Penance and Reconciliation

On the first Easter Sunday Jesus gave His Apostles a very wonderful and great power.

It was the power to forgive our sins.

Jesus gave this power to His Apostles.

They were His first priests.

Through the Apostles Jesus gives this power to all priests.

In the sacrament of Penance and Reconciliation the priest uses this power.

In the sacrament of Penance and Reconciliation I tell my sins to the priest.

My sins are forgiven by the priest if I am sorry for them.

Jesus is God.
Jesus knows all I think.
Jesus knows all I do.
Jesus knows all I say.
I cannot keep a secret from Jesus.
Jesus knows when I sin.
Jesus knows when I am sorry for my sins.
Jesus hears my prayers and forgives me when we I tell him that I am sorry.
I must also tell my sins to the priest in confession.
The priest represents Jesus.
In confession I receive God's mercy and live again in the grace of His Church.
I will try my best not to displease our Lord by my sins.
In confession the priest uses the power Jesus gives him.
I must never be afraid to tell my sins to the priest.
I will listen to everything the priest says.
He will be kind to me and help me.
The priest will keep my sins a secret.
When I tell my sins to the priest in confession I am really telling them to Jesus.
Through the priest, Jesus forgives me my sins.
The sins are then gone from my soul.
I will do or say the penance that the priest gives me.
Jesus was very kind to me when He gave His priests this great power to forgive me my sins.
I can never thank Jesus enough for this gift of the sacrament of Penance and Reconciliation.
I must remember to pray for the priest who takes my sins away.

Catechism Lesson

117. What is the sacrament of Penance and Reconciliation?

Penance and Reconciliation is the sacrament by which sins committed after Baptism are forgiven.

118. When did Jesus give us the sacrament of Penance and Reconciliation?

Jesus gave us the sacrament of Penance and Reconciliation on Easter Sunday night.

119. When do I receive the sacrament of Penance and Reconciliation?

I receive the sacrament of Penance and Reconciliation when I go to confession.

120. What is confession?

Confession is the telling of my sins to a priest so as to be forgiven.

121. What must you do to receive the sacrament of Penance and Reconciliation worthily?

To receive the sacrament of Penance and Reconciliation worthily I must:

1. Call to mind my sins.
2. Be sorry for my sins.
3. Make up my mind not to sin again.
4. Tell my sins to the priest.
5. Do the penance the priest gives me.

122. How do you make your confession?

I make my confession in this way:

1. I go into the confessional and kneel.
2. I make the sign of the cross and say: "Bless me, Father, for I have sinned."
3. I say: "This is my first confession" (or, "It has been one week, or one month, since my last confession").
4. I confess my sins.
5. I listen to what the priest tells me.
6. I say the act of contrition aloud.

123. What do you do after leaving the confessional?

After leaving the confessional, I say the penance the priest has given me and thank God for forgiving my sins.

124. Does the priest keep your confession a secret?

Yes, the priest always keeps my confession a secret.

UNIT 5

How God Cares for Our Souls Through the Holy Eucharist

CHAPTER 22
The Holy Eucharist

One day when Jesus was at a wedding He changed water into wine.

Another time He fed a crowd of hungry people.

He gave them food for their bodies.

On another day, He promised them food for their souls.

Jesus said to the people, "I am the living bread that has come down from heaven."

Jesus kept this promise when He gave us the sacrament of Holy Eucharist.

Jesus gave us this sacrament at the Last Supper, the night before He died.

The Holy Eucharist is the living Body, Blood, Soul, and Divinity of Jesus Christ.

The priest changes bread and wine into the Body and Blood of Jesus at Mass.

The Holy Eucharist looks like bread.

The Holy Eucharist tastes like bread.

But the Holy Eucharist is *not* bread.

The Holy Eucharist is Jesus.

Jesus gives Himself to me in the Holy Eucharist.

Jesus is the Food of my soul.

Catechism Lesson

125. What is the sacrament of the Holy Eucharist?
The Holy Eucharist is the sacrament of the Body and Blood of our Lord Jesus Christ.

126. When did Christ institute (give us) the Holy Eucharist?
Christ instituted (gave us) the Holy Eucharist at the Last Supper, the night before He died.

127. What did our Lord do at the Last Supper?
At the Last Supper our Lord changed bread and wine into His real Body and Blood.

128. How could our Lord change bread and wine into His Body and Blood?
Our Lord could do this because He is God, and God can do all things.

129. Who were with our Lord at the Last Supper?
The Apostles were with our Lord at the Last Supper.

130. Did our Lord give the Apostles and priests the power to change bread and wine into His Body and Blood?
Our Lord gave the Apostles and all the priests of the Catholic Church the power to change bread and wine into His Body and Blood.

131. When do the priests use this power?
The priests use this power when they offer Holy Mass.

CHAPTER 23

The Mass

At the Last Supper Jesus offered the first Mass.
The Apostles were with Jesus when He said the first Mass.
Jesus took bread in His hands and said, "This is My Body."
Jesus took a cup of wine and said, "This is My Blood."
At once the bread and wine became the real living Body and Blood of Jesus.
Then Jesus gave His Body to His Apostles to eat, and His Blood to drink.
When Jesus said to the Apostles, "Do this in remembrance of Me," He made them His first priests.
He gave them the power to offer Mass.
The Apostles and all the priests of the Catholic Church have used this power ever since.
The priests do as Jesus did at the Last Supper.
They do this when they offer Mass.
Jesus offered Himself to His heavenly Father.
He gave His life for us on the cross.
The Mass is the same sacrifice as that of the cross.

ON THE CROSS:	Jesus, true High Priest, offered Himself to God the Father.
AT MASS:	Jesus offers Himself to God the Father through the priest.
ON THE CROSS:	Jesus was the Victim.
AT MASS:	Jesus is the Victim.
ON THE CROSS:	Jesus gave His life for all people.
AT MASS:	The life of Jesus is again offered for all people.

During Mass I can offer many gifts to God. God gives many gifts to me.

At the *Offertory* the priest offers the bread and wine to God.
At the Offertory I must offer myself to God.
I offer God my love, prayers, work, and play.
I want to give God all that I am and all that I have.

The *Consecration* is the holiest part of the Mass.
At the Consecration of the Mass, the priest says, "This is My Body."

This changes the bread into Jesus.
He says: "This is My Blood."
This changes the wine into His Blood.
Jesus offers Himself to God for us.
I cannot see Jesus but I know He is there.
The priest raises the Sacred Host and the Chalice above his head.
I look up and say, "My Lord and my God."

At the *Communion* of the Mass God has a Gift for me.
This Gift is Jesus in Holy Communion.
The priest receives Jesus in Holy Communion.
I receive Jesus in Holy Communion.
I receive Him for the first time on my First Communion Day.
Jesus will come to me in Holy Communion every day if I want Him.

Catechism Lesson

132. What is the Mass?

The Mass is the offering to God the Father of our Lord's Body and Blood.

133. When was the first Mass offered?
The first Mass was offered at the Last Supper.

134. Who offers Mass for us?
The priests of the Catholic Church offer Mass for us and with us.

135. Is the Mass the same as the Last Supper?
The Mass is the same as the Last Supper because the priest changes bread and wine into our Lord's Body and Blood when he says, "This is My Body; This is My Blood."

136. Why do we offer the Holy Mass?
We offer the Holy Mass:

1. to adore God.
2. to thank God.
3. to ask God for what we need.
4. to tell God we are sorry for our sins.

137. Must we be present for the whole Mass on Sundays and holy days of obligation?
Yes, we must be present for the whole Mass on Sundays and holy days of obligation. We commit a grave sin if through our own fault we are not present for the three principal parts of the Mass.

138. What are the three principal parts of the Mass?
The three principal parts of the Mass are:

1. the Offertory.
2. the Consecration.
3. the Communion.

CHAPTER 24
Holy Communion

Jesus loves me.
Jesus wants to come to me often in Holy Communion.
I must get ready for Jesus to come to me.
I am ready when I am God's friend and have His life in me.
I am ready when I tell Jesus I am sorry for my sins.
I am ready when I tell Jesus that I love Him and want Him to come to me.
I am ready when I do not eat or drink anything but water for one hour before receiving Communion.

When Jesus comes to me I will thank Him.
I will tell Him how happy I am that He is with me.
I will tell Him that I believe He is both God and man.
I will tell Him that I love Him.
I will tell Him that I hope to live with Him in heaven some day.
I will ask Him to bless and help everyone on earth and in purgatory.
I will ask Him to love me and stay with me always.

Catechism Lesson

139. What is Holy Communion?

Holy Communion is the receiving of our Lord's Body and Blood.

140. Do you see Jesus Christ in the Holy Eucharist?

No, I do not see Jesus Christ in the Holy Eucharist because He is hidden under the appearances of bread and wine.

141. What must you do to receive Holy Communion?

To receive Holy Communion I must:

1. Have my soul free from mortal sin.
2. Not eat or drink anything for one hour before Holy Communion. But water may be taken at any time before Holy Communion.

142. What should you do before Holy Communion?

Before Holy Communion I should:

1. think of Jesus.
2. say the prayers I have learned.
3. ask Jesus to come to me.

143. What should you do after Holy Communion?

After Holy Communion I should:

1. thank Jesus for coming to me.
2. tell Him how much I love Him.
3. ask Him to help me.
4. pray for others.

Prayers

The Sign of the Cross

In the name of the Father, and of the Son, and of the Holy Spirit. Amen.

The Lord's Prayer

Our Father who art in heaven,
Hallowed be Thy name;
Thy kingdom come;
Thy will be done on earth as it is in heaven.
Give us this day our daily bread;
And forgive us our trespasses as we forgive those who trespass against us;
And lead us not into temptation,
But deliver us from evil. Amen.

The Hail Mary

Hail Mary, full of grace! the Lord is with thee; blessed art thou among women, and blessed is the fruit of thy womb, Jesus. Holy Mary, Mother of God, pray for us sinners, now and at the hour of our death. Amen.

Glory Be to the Father

Glory be to the Father, and to the Son, and to the Holy Spirit. As it was in the beginning, is now, and ever shall be, world without end. Amen.

The Apostles' Creed

I believe in God, the Father almighty, Creator of heaven and earth, and in Jesus Christ, His only Son, Our Lord, who was conceived by the Holy Spirit, born of the Virgin Mary, suffered under Pontius Pilate, was crucified, died and was buried; He descended into hell; on the third day He rose again from the dead; He ascended into heaven, and is seated at the right hand of God the Father almighty; from there He will come to judge the living and the dead. I believe in the Holy Spirit, the holy Catholic Church, the communion of saints, the forgiveness of sins, the resurrection of the body, and life everlasting. Amen.

An Act of Faith

O my God, I believe all the truths which the Holy Catholic Church teaches, because Thou hast made them known.

An Act of Hope

O my God, because Thou art all-powerful, merciful, and faithful to Thy promises, I hope to be happy with Thee in heaven.

An Act Of Love

O my God, because Thou art all-good, I love Thee with my whole heart and soul.

Prayer to the Guardian Angel

Angel of God, my guardian dear, to whom His love entrusts me here, ever this day be at my side, to light and guard, to rule and guide. Amen.

An Act of Contrition

O my God, I am heartily sorry for having offended Thee, and I detest all my sins, because of Thy just punishments, but most of all because they offend Thee, my God, Who art all-good and deserving of all my love. I firmly resolve, with the help of Thy grace, to sin no more and to avoid the near occasions of sin. Amen.

Prayer to the Holy Spirit Before Confession

Come, Holy Spirit, enlighten my mind, strengthen my will, that I may know my sins, be truly sorry for them, and humbly confess them.

The Morning Offering

O Jesus, through the Immaculate Heart of Mary, I offer Thee my prayers, works, joys, and sufferings of this day for all the intentions of Thy Sacred Heart, in union with the Holy Sacrifice of the Mass throughout the world, in reparation for my sins, for the intentions of all our relatives and friends, and in particular for the intentions of the Holy Father. Amen.

Blessing Before Meals

Bless us, O Lord, and these Thy gifts which we are about to receive from Thy bounty, through Christ our Lord. Amen.

Grace After Meals

We give Thee thanks for all Thy benefits, O almighty God, Who lives and reigns forever. Amen.
May the souls of the faithful departed, through the mercy of God, rest in peace. Amen.

The Divine Praises

Blessed be God.
Blessed be His holy name.
Blessed Be Jesus Christ, true God and true Man.
Blessed be the name of Jesus.
Blessed be His most Sacred Heart.
Blessed be Jesus in the most holy Sacrament of the Altar.
Blessed be the great Mother of God, Mary most holy.
Blessed be her holy and Immaculate Conception.
Blessed be her glorious Assumption.
Blessed be the name of Mary, Virgin and Mother.
Blessed be St. Joseph, her most chaste spouse.
Blessed be God in His angels and in His saints.

Short Prayers to Remember

1. My Jesus, mercy.
2. Most Sacred Heart of Jesus, have mercy on us.
3. Immaculate Heart of Mary, pray for us now, and at the hour of our death.
4. Eternal rest grant unto them, O Lord, and let perpetual light shine upon them. May they rest in peace. Amen.
5. O Mary, conceived without sin, pray for us, who have recourse to thee.

6. My God, I love Thee.
7. O God, be merciful to me, a sinner.
8. O Sacrament most holy, O Sacrament divine! All praise and all thanksgiving be every moment Thine!
9. Jesus, Mary, Joseph.
10. My Lord and my God.
11. We adore Thee, O Christ, and we bless Thee because by Thy holy cross, Thou hast redeemed the world.

Suggested Prayers for First Communion Day

Prayers Before Holy Communion

Dear Jesus, because Thou hast said it, I believe that I shall receive Thee in the Sacrament of Thy Love.

I believe this with all my heart.

Sweet Jesus, help me to make a good Communion.

Mary, my dearest Mother, pray to Jesus for me.

My dear Angel Guardian, lead me to the altar of God.

Dear Jesus, I love Thee.

I thank Thee for being here.

I adore Thee.

I desire with all my heart to receive Thee.

Come, dear Jesus, give me Thy Body, Blood, Soul, and Divinity.

Come, dear Jesus, come.

Prayers After Holy Communion

Jesus, my God, I believe You are truly present in this sacrament of Thy love.

I praise You.

I adore You.

I thank You for coming to me.

I love You with my whole heart; help me to love You more.

Dear Jesus, how happy I am that You have come to me.

I want to give myself to You.

I give You my soul and body.

I give You all that I am and all that I have.

I will use my tongue to praise You and to speak kindly of others.

I will use my hands to do good things.

I will do all things to please You.

Dear Jesus, bless my father and mother.

Bless all the people for whom I have prayed during this Holy Mass.

Bless me and help me to live as a child of God.

I want You to stay with me always.